That Ain't Nothing New (But Does it Matter?)

That Ain't Nothing New (But Does it Matter?)

The Genius of Business Ideas Rediscovered

L. David Harris

Harris Author Services

Contents

Special Thanks

Big shout to my literary alter ego, "Adam," who helps me to get some of my secular ideas into print while I continue to work hard on my spiritual books. He makes DavidWritesA-Lot.com a more efficient machine.

I have published a novella about this mystery character appropriately titled, "Adam: My Literary Alter Ego." Get your copy today!

Introduction

Hotel California, the popular rock music song from the late 1970s, which is still revered and widely listened to until now, was stolen! That's right, the Eagles copied the song. In 2009, the song was certified Platinum – Digital Sales Award, by the Recording Industry Association of America (RIAA) for selling over a million copies, downloaded digitally. *Hotel California* topped Billboard charts in 1977 and was ranked number 49 on "The 500 Greatest Songs of All Time", a list compiled by the highly esteemed Rolling Stones magazine. But, the song was burglarized and no one seems to care, heaping accolades for the song and its writers' decades after the original release.

Ian Anderson, lead singer of an old band, Jethro Tull, acknowledged that the Eagles had toured with his band in the early 1970s and it is not a mere coincidence that the popular "Hotel California" song displays striking similarities to Jethro Tull's song "We Used to Know." Anderson showed great poise while discussing the uncanny resemblance between the two songs, arguing the Eagles may have internalized the song and then subconsciously re-introduced the musical tune in their popular "Hotel California" song.

He goes on to state it's highly unlikely to discover a chord sequence, which hasn't been previously played. It's almost guaranteed mathematically that if you play a guitar looking for something new, you will eventually string together bits of old tunes rearranged to form your song. Inventions in all other

1

spheres of life take the same route as innovations in the music industry.

There are rarely ever brand "new" ideas. Inventions are often old ideas recycled, enhanced and marketed in a new method and format. This is all called freewheeling innovation and this is how society (and technology) progresses. You cannot be afraid to take someone else's ideas, improve on it and claim the idea as your own. This "thievery" is almost the lifeline of innovation.

Recent technological advancements have been mostly regulated to the corporate level, but inter-corporate dealings prove the freewheeling innovation theory. Corporate giants are constantly confronting each other in front of judges, arguing about whether one firm has copied technology invented by another firm. If nothing else, this proves to you and me that copying others is a hallmark of inventions.

Now, if only our courts would understand this concept, the little guys would have a much better chance. Corporations are constantly copying each other's ideas and improving upon them. They also have the resources to defend their improvements in court, unlike most individuals, who cannot fight against a litany of highly remunerated, bloodthirsty corporate lawyers.

Yet, you cannot and should not let this hold you back as the only chance you have to being sued is if you have successfully introduced something "new" which is actually hurting sales of a big corporate monster. A lawsuit against you will only confirm your success. The notion that new ideas and products are invented is just a creation myth. Whether it's the progress of ideas or tangible products, supposedly "new" concepts are almost always derived from old concepts.

1

Theft is the Thrust of Innovation

The history of innovation is littered with "new" ideas, which were often the result of improvement on past technologies. But, we don't need to delve too far back in history. Everyone is in agreement that progress in the modern era is increasing in leaps and bounds because scientific information is so widely disseminated. Therefore, since the current era is at the top of the list of the number of inventions versus any other era, we decided to analyze some revolutionary ideas of our time and where they were "stolen" from.

Steve Jobs is probably the most recognized face on the planet when it comes to consumer development in personal computing and many felt his death was untimely, coming too early and preventing us from seeing his true genius. He is attributed to have invented many revolutionizing products and we wholeheartedly agree. However, we just want to point out his inventions were stolen from others, before being re-worked and re-introduced to the world as a new invention. His brilliance lies in the fact he didn't invent anything new at all, he just re-invented old items.

Mouse and Graphical User Interface

In the mid-1980's, Apple unveiled its iconic Macintosh computer, an invention which transformed the personal computing industry altogether. There were two important features of this revolutionary device: the Graphical User Interface (GUI) and the mouse. How did Apple invent these ideas is a tale which must be told countless times to remind people of a simple yet absolutely true fact: Innovation is stolen ideas, re-packaged for success.

The Story

Although it may read like modern folklore, this is a story based in fact and it explains the legend that is Steve Jobs.

In 1979, a boisterous 24-year old entrepreneur with a small startup company of his own in Silicon Valley negotiated an extraordinary deal. The man was Steve Jobs, co-founder of Apple. His company was in its initial stages, but it had already garnered the attention of the industry. Its Initial Public Offering (IPO) was still a year away, but it was highly anticipated and everyone wanted a piece of it.

At this time, there was also a well-known company called Xerox, with a division titled PARC. The 1970s belonged to PARC and its innovations. Any American engineer wanting a glimpse of the future craved a peek into PARC's research lab, the innovative arm of Xerox, tucked away from management so they could let their creative juices flow freely. Steve Jobs wanted a piece of that future and he was willing to gamble a high price to get it.

Jobs negotiated with Xerox's top management and convinced them to buy 100,000 shares of Apple for a million dollars in exchange of letting him snoop around the top research facility for computer engineering and programming in the country and run by Xerox.

Steve Jobs and Bill Atkinson, a software engineer at Apple,

were given a couple of tours of the secretive facility. They ended up staring at Alto, PARC's version of a personal computer. Larry Tesler, a PARC engineer carried out the presentation of Alto. He used a "mouse" to move an on-screen cursor to click on icons, open and close programs, and work with a word-processing software. He also exchanged "emails" internally on the first Ethernet network in the world.

Amidst all the technological innovations they got to peek at, Jobs and Atkinson were transfixed by the personal computer. Atkinson zoomed in to the screen to the point that his nose was almost touching the monitor. After a minute of keen observation, Jobs couldn't contain his excitement. He was hopping around the room screaming, "Why aren't you doing anything with this? This is the greatest thing. This is revolutionary!" This gave birth to the legend of Jobs.

Back at Apple headquarters, Job told his team he wanted to create the next generation personal computer, a device which he had already witnessed in operation at Xerox, yet his company is still attributed with its invention.

A final word on the mouse is that even Xerox employees at PARC didn't really invent it and they too stole the idea. The victim was Douglas Engelbart, a computer scientist at Stanford's research institute. In the mid-1960's, Engelbart conceived the idea of moving a "signal" (cursor) on the screen with the use of a separate mechanical device. He came up with a rectangular, bulky and roller-skate wheel look-alike contraption. Unfortunately, we cannot go back and ask Engelbart from where he spied his idea, but we can say it's highly likely that he too was inspired by something he saw in nature or man-made which made him produce his mouse. This is the nature of innovation. It evolves from one stage to the next and at the root of it is the theory that your new idea will be stolen from a pre-existing concept.

The iPad

Another popular Apple invention also stolen from competitors was the iPad, launched in 2010. At the time, critics felt Apple had run out of innovative ideas and was just creating a large iPhone. In a sense they were correct, because Apple had never invented anything. They were just good at re-hashing old ideas in a new innovative fashion. But more to the point, Apple hadn't run out of innovations: they had just found a new niche. By the end of 2015, they will have sold just fewer than three hundred million iPads. The evolution of the personal digital assistant (PDA) from its beginning to the launch of the iPad will highlight how ideas which evolve are copied from one step to the next.

The History

Apple may have introduced the iPad in 2010, but that is almost a quarter century after the appearance of the first handwriting-recognizing device.

1987

The Linus Write-Top was unveiled in 1987 and allowed users to use its stylus to write on a green screen.

1989

Palm Computing launched the GridPad two year after the Linus Write-Top. Some experts in the field title the GridPad as the first official tablet computer. It was run on MS-DOS and the military found it useful so they bought a few, but people mostly ignored it due to its high price and heavy load. The GridPad weighed a lot as compared to the laptops available at the time.

1993

Apple's first foray into the tablet market proved to be such a disastrous failure no one even remembers they tried to create a tablet before the iPad became a revolutionary product. It was called Newton MessagePad and Apple's intent was to create a new device category (PDA) without shrinking sales from its personal computer market. The MessagePad came pre-loaded with "apps" to create a to-do list and a calendar. You could input data on it with a stylus, which was supposed to recognize your handwriting, but the technology was not quite successful.

1997

The first PDA that was actually successful was inaugurated by Jeff Hawkins, also responsible for the 1989 GridPad. It was cleverly called the PalmPilot and was the first affordable PDA. PalmPilot's successors would eventually move to touch screens and become quite popular. There was finally proof consumers were in the need for a third type of device, something in between a laptop and a cell phone, which had to be affordable and simple to utilize.

2000

Apple archrival, Microsoft's Bill Gates unveiled his tablet computer in 2000. This was probably the first time a PDA device was described as a tablet and many people credit Bill Gates and Microsoft for coining the term. Gates was about five years off when he predicted in 2000 tablets would be big business in five years.

2002

Microsoft didn't give up too easily when the Tablet PC of 2000 didn't take off as they expected. They developed a tablet version of Windows XP and induced a few PC makers to produce the Windows XP Tablet. Compaq manufactured one and so did Fujitsu. Still, Microsoft was a little too early or didn't have the right specs to entice a mass audience to purchase these devices.

Mid-2000s

It seems the personal computing industry took notice after Microsoft introduced a tablet in 2000 and another one in 2002, even though consumers didn't make any attachment to the devices. In the mid-2000s there were numerous tablet options available to the consumer. The LS800 designed collaboratively by Lenovo ThinkPad and Motion Computing was an interesting option. It was the smallest tablet on the market at the time at 8.4 inches, but cost a hefty $2,167. The price was too prohibitive to appeal to the masses and such devices were mostly utilized by the military or in factories.

2010

This was the year when the iPad finally graced us with its presence. It may have been a new invention to most of us, but by now we hope you are seeing the pattern. The iPad was just a stolen idea, improved upon and re-introduced as brand new to the masses. Innovation is stealing. This was, by the way, the second time Apple had ventured into the tablet market so another important lesson is don't give up too early.

Perhaps if Microsoft would have continued with their efforts after the 2002 Windows XP Tablet, they would have been the ones reaping success of the tablet market. However, timing is often an important issue when it comes to innovating successful ideas.

World Wide Web

A final idea which is a great example of how ideas evolve one to another and innovation relies on stealing concepts already in existence is that of the Internet.

Inventor

The creation of the World Wide Web is credited to one man: Tim Berners-Lee. The general public views this man as the person who enabled our digital lives with his break-through invention. However, scientists and experts in the field realize he was just the final piece of the long puzzle of minor improvements and alterations to existing technologies, which came together and helped create the Internet. The important Internet concept of hyperlinks (or gateways to other locations) had been investigated by researchers at Brown University and engineers at Apple before it was incorporated into the Internet idea.

Initial Purpose

A major catalyst for the creation of the Internet was the Cold War. When the Soviets launched the Sputnik satellite into outer space, the Americans realized they needed to stop worrying about building better and bigger cars and concentrate on innovation if they want to succeed against the USSR. The government created agencies tasked with developing technologies, giving birth to the well-recognized NASA and a little less known ARPA (Advanced Research Project Agency), the research arm of the American Department of Defense. A major concern at the time was the Communists could fairly easily disable America's network of phone systems and there was a need to create an alternate communication network.

The Start

An ARPA scientist proposed in 1962 a "virtual" network, which would enable computers to link to each other and allow people to communicate through them, preventing communication failures among government leaders if the Russians attacked the telephone system.

First Practical Steps

The first communication between computers occurred in 1965 when a M.I.T. researcher came up with the idea of "packet switching", which involved the computer breaking data in packets and sending the packet to another destination. In 1969, the first message was communicated between two computers (one was located at UCLA and the other at Stanford), which had dimensions similar to that of a small home. The message communicated was "login", but the network was overloaded and crashed after delivering only the first two letters. Yet, it was considered a successful start.

Network Growth

The networks grew steadily till 1971 with more computers connected to each other yearly, but it became tedious to maintain different connections and researchers attempted to discover a method to link them all on a single worldwide network, the "Internet".

A Singular Network

By the late 1970s, a computer scientist helped solve this issue by creating Transmission Control Protocol (TCP) and later Internet Protocol (IP), currently known as TCP/IP. This enabled different computers to communicate to each other in "virtual" space on a single worldwide network. During the 1980s, scientists and researchers used this network to send files to each other through their computers.

Birth of the Internet

In 1991, the Swiss Berners-Lee created the World Wide Web, a network which not only allowed users to send files to each other, but a virtual location where information was available for retrieval. Anyone with access to the Internet could read this "web" of information. In 1992, the American Congress passed a bill allowing the Internet to be used as a commercial tool and ushering a wave of web development technologies.

Current Version

The final step to arrive at the Internet as we know it today was the creation in 1992 of user-friendly method to browse the information available on the Internet. A team of students from the University of Illinois developed a program they called Mosaic (later known as Netscape). This enabled Internet users to search for it more easily for information, which was then displayed in an easy to read fashion. It was now to possible to view pictures and words on the same "webpage", which could have clickable links and scrollbars to help a browser navigate the Internet more easily.

At the start of this process, the idea was never to build an Internet, although this is where consecutive evolutions led.

Subsequent scientists and researchers took ideas from each other and improved on them. Although, there is one person known for creating the Internet, it was a series of improvements, which led to this innovation.

2

Generating Ideas

There are wonderful stories that support the light-bulb moment, which signifies the ushering of an absolutely new and fascinating idea into the world. This light-bulb moment concept may be an excellent plotline for Hollywood movies, but does a disservice to progress by giving people the impression that you may one day just happen upon a brilliant idea which will enrich you beyond your imagination.

New ideas are not only derived from old processes and innovations, but they require you to actively think about creating something new by improving upon the old. Your mind has to be trained to view products and concepts critically to be able to build upon them by improving shortcomings in existing ideas, products and services.

Just like you may have heard of a product's lifecycle, ideas also have their particular lifecycle. Good ideas happen not in light-bulb moments, but by organizing and collaborating with others. They happen by letting yourself being influenced by other cultures and processes, and with the help of intuition.

Dedication

Innovation is not an overnight project so don't hit the rubber running, but rather start at a slow but dedicated pace. You need to train your mind to be constantly critical of everything surrounding you. This may sound negative, but it doesn't mean you should be continuously criticizing everyone and everything around you.

If you do this, you will project a negative outlook on life and it would make you a horrible person to socialize with. The real purpose is to get your mind ready to look for processes, ideas, products and services that can be improved upon. It's more about having a critical inner thought rather being critical of everything. For instance, when you use a product you like (or dislike), think about how it can be improved. This actually is about putting a positive spin on things.

Sounding Board

Constantly trying to re-hash ideas with a new outlook on them will not get you too far without some feedback. Another misconception the light-bulb notion disperses is that ideas are often coined by a single individual. You can throw out this concept fairly easily. The best ideas are those which are generated by collaborating with others. Steve Jobs set some parameters, but it was his engineers who came up with the prototypes. They worked together to create the next big project, not as individuals.

Recruit a close friend or relative. You can even sign up your significant other. All you need is a supportive ear who will listen to your ideas. Even if the person does not give you much feedback, having the opportunity to talk out your ideas loudly will allow you to view them in a different angle. You may gradually come to realize if your idea should be dumped, or how it can be improved. On the other hand, a person who shares your sense of wonderment about stealing a new idea may help you get to your goal more quickly with helpful observations.

No Judgment

While you and your sounding board are in the process of generating ideas, it is imperative to leave your judgmental side at the checkout counter. You need to have a critical mind to help you improve upon others' ideas and products, but do not start judging how useless or horrible your ideas are at this stage. The more ideas you can generate, the greater the possibility you will discover one that will be successful. Don't be cowered by the thought that the idea could work, but may require a great deal of capital or it's just too wild. It's possible to scale down successful ideas, but impossible to successfully scale up bad ideas.

Patience

Ideas take time and you need to be patient with this process. There will be a moment when all of a sudden something just feels right and in this sense, the light-bulb concept is actually fairly accurate. As explained above, it will take time and effort to arrive at that moment. Steve Jobs' iconic words remind you to trust yourself when he said "intuition is a powerful thing, more powerful than intellect, in my opinion." You may be stealing someone's idea, but it will still be new to the world and so you will never positively know before-hand if the idea will be successful or not. You will have to trust your gut and jump in with both feet if your intuition is telling you have hit the goldmine.

Experience

Our pop culture has fed us the idea it's possible to come up with a brilliantly revolutionary (and money generating) idea as a pimple-face, starry eyed 20-year old working out of a garage, your parent's basement or a dorm room. If you quit an Ivy League university, you exponentially improve your success chances (billionaire entrepreneurs Bill Gates, Steve Jobs, Michael Dell, Mark Zuckerberg and the list goes on) and are billed as extremely confident and fashionably entrepreneurial that you can achieve success even if you are selling milk from a roadside stall.

It's time to prick the bubble of this business myth and let the bursting sound awaken (or perhaps enlighten) your senses. Rebels and the inexperienced don't always succeed in generating big business ideas and there's a lot of proof to counter this false cultural image.

A garage or basement conjures the image of a lone young and inexperienced person or two working on a singularly dedicated effort to create a product or idea and who will overcame all obstacles on their path to success. This narrative is counterproductive to innovation since it is rarely a reality. A research out of UC Berkeley's School of Business demystified this quixotic idea in a recent study. The paper found some of the most successful CEOs of innovative corporations, whether it is in their products, processes or services were groomed in business organizations.

Another study of venture capital financed enterprises concluded 91% of founders of such companies were in an industry in which they had prior experience. They were not simpletons, lacking knowledge and experience and triumphing over challenges through sheer effort and talent, but were men who had polished their skills in various organizations and had left these organizations to form their start-ups. Young rebels don't make the best entrepreneurs, but rather it is people with experience.

Take the myth of YouTube founders, Chad Hurley and Steve Chen. The popular unofficial plotline is of a couple of twenty-year old genius buddies working together to create a website which could help them easily exchange videos with friends on the Internet. In reality, Chen was also a PayPal employee and Hurley had joined PayPal so early in its operations that he is the one who designed their logo. He also happens to be James Clark's son-in-law. Clark started Netscape and Silicon Graphics, so not only did Hurley get to cut his teeth in a successful Internet start-up, but he could draw upon the experience of a successful CEO in the IT industry.

Chen and Hurley were well-known in the industry and within months of launching YouTube, venture capitalists were calling them, offering networking opportunities, advice and most importantly plenty of financing at a time when corporations often fail, not because their idea isn't great, but they do not have the financial resources to get through the difficult initial stages when budgets and money are tight.

Pop culture did get the garage part right when it comes to Wozniak, Jobs and Apple, though, what it omits is more important. Wozniak was an engineer at Hewlett-Packard and Jobs was employee number 40 at Atari and also sharpened his skills at HP. The reality then is that great ideas and companies don't have their beginnings in basements or garages. Rather, their birth takes place in other corporations.

This reality check may feel like it lessens the value of success achieved by the aforementioned people. It takes away from the storied legend of broke, young, inexperienced, rebellious university dropout entrepreneurs rising from ashes like a phoenix and replaces it with a more accurate account of a startup company which surfaced after networking with industry experts and identifying market opportunities which could be exploited to financial gain while the meetings were held in lavish conference rooms at a Novotel Hotel. Boring! Who wouldn't be gullible to believing the myth about garages and innovation if this is reality?

It's more fun to believe Christopher Columbus wanted to prove an earth shattering concept which no one would entertain at his time and called him a heretic for suggesting the world is round and you could in theory sail west to reach India. That he had an enormously difficult time recruiting crewmembers that were scared away when they found out they were going to the edge of the world. This is the version which excites us and the one we want Hollywood to portray, but in fact, most people at that time already believed the Earth was round and Columbus didn't want to reach India, but was on the hunt for a little glitter: Gold!

Over time, these glamorous stories take a life of their own and the legend grows, creating this myth about amazing personalities with brilliant minds who overcame great odds on their path to success. Don't let these stories derail your thoughts of finding an idea to improve upon and reintroduce to the world. Great ideas take a lot of time and purposeful effort. They evolve step-by-step and require expertise, knowledge and experience. If you want to innovate a new idea one day, start by getting a job.

3

Innovation Challenges

Just like any other aspect of your life, innovation and invention carries its own sets of risks and rewards. When you have engaged your mind to copying the great next product, you have to expect some challenges. If you do, the rewards will be even better.

Constraints May Create More

Once you have found your idea, you can create constraints to make it appeal to the masses. For instance, Steve Jobs knew the mouse was an innovative product, but he added additional constraints that allowed him to significantly change the copied idea and call it his own, while at the same time creating a product which could be easily used by the average personal computer consumer.

His mouse project was only successful because he challenged his engineers with seemingly impossible limitations. The Xerox mouse cost over $300, while Mr. Jobs envisioned a $15 mouse. He wanted one button on the mouse with even more functionalities than the three-button Xerox mouse. This may seem like contradictory logic, but Steve Jobs didn't let constraints scare him. He let them improve his ideas.

Failure: A Prerequisite to Success

When looking at current products and processes and thinking about how to re-hash to make them new to the world, you will think of a dozen ideas which will not be worth the paper you write your ideas on. This is a process, which will lead you to success, because it is extremely rare for anyone to be successful on their first try. Failures help you learn from your mistakes. You realize what doesn't work and how to change certain features to enhance your probabilities of success.

Big Picture

In a corporate environment, it is well known by engineers that just because they think they have an amazing money-generating idea does not necessarily mean they will receive the financing to explore their idea and bring it to fruition. High-level management often has a myopic view rather than explore the idea to discover if there is real potential. They will look at the cost of the exploration and decide to dump the idea. In other words, they will not search for a potential goldmine because the shovel is too expensive.

When you are trying to recycle an idea and re-introduce it to the market, it is important to avoid this pitfall. There are times when prudent fiscal planning is absolutely necessary, but it is not at that time when your intuition strongly tells you may be about to hit the jackpot. The point here is not to bankrupt yourself while chasing your dream, because just as we acknowledge dreams are worth all our efforts, money is the engine which powers that pursuit.

If you feel the financial burden placed upon you and your family will be too great to handle, it may be time to bring in an outside investor. This will grant you two benefits. The first obvious one is a cash infusion and the second one is that you will get a second critical eye, which will help guide your steps towards creating the perfect new stolen idea.

Inside the Box

To find the great next stolen idea, you don't have to constantly think outside the box. Remember, innovation is just a progression of ideas. You don't have to pull something out of thin air. Rather, your idea already exists somewhere on this planet. This implies the more you deal with everyday items, the greater probability you have of finding a product or idea to improve upon and call it your own invention.

Field of Expertise

When Steve Jobs went to tour Xerox's PARC facility, he must have seen numerous projects in various stages of development, but the idea he felt would revolutionize the world was the GUI and the mouse. This begs the question of why did he instantly recognize these as ideas worth investing into? Simply because personal computing was his background experience and it was the project they were already working on at Apple.

Steve Jobs already knew in-depth everything there was to know about the personal computing industry. He knew the extent of technology available, the size of the market and the shortcomings in the technology. He probably had studied all these ideas in detail and he was mentally ready for an idea to help solve a problem, so when he saw the mouse and GUI at PARC, it was his light-bulb moment.

Conversely, PARC was a highly creative institute, operating at arm's length from business bureaucrats to specifically avoid a stifling imaginative environment, where all possibilities were considered and promoted. It was staffed by some of the brightest and forward thinking engineers at Xerox and probably in the US.

How come then, these highly sophisticated engineers and developers, didn't see the potential Steve Jobs foretold the moment he saw the mouse and GUI operated by Xerox at PARC? Again, the answer lies in a person's field of expertise. Xerox engineers didn't have the experience Steve Jobs had with personal computing. They didn't know what was lacking in that domain and what could revolutionize it so they overlooked the potential of the mouse and GUI they had invented.

This argument is made even more poignant when you analyze it in the context of a few dates. 1979 was the year Steve Jobs was given a tour of PARC, the year in which he jumped up and down in their facility telling them they have the greatest revolutionary product and asking them why they aren't doing anything with this technology. It's not as if he toured the company and quietly left without giving a hint to PARC engineers of what he liked.

No, he made it abundantly clear what he would be working on. 1984 was the year Apple unveiled its Macintosh computer with a GUI and mouse that was reminiscent of the items he saw at PARC. This was a five-year time span in which PARC and Xerox engineers could have brought the product to market, as they were already told this was revolutionary.

In 1981, Xerox put out a personal computer on the market, which eventually failed and Xerox pulled out of the industry completely. As they did not have extensive knowledge of the market, they didn't know what would make them successful

even after it was pointed out to them. Experience and expertise in a particular field is therefore a key to innovation.

4

First Movers and Fast Followers

The timing of an innovation is an important aspect to consider as it has a tremendous impact on a new idea's chances of success. Sometimes, a "first mover" company will do exceptionally well when they are the first to introduce a product to consumers, whereas at other times it is best to wait out the initial period and build a better product based on consumer feedback and then reap greater rewards as a "fast follower". It is important to analyze when and why each theory may be more successful so you may launch your stolen idea at the appropriate time.

First Movers

The theory states a company or product, which establishes itself first in a particular industry, gains a competitive advantage over later entrants in the market. This is because the first company is able to capture a large percentage of market share, build brand recognition, and gain customer loyalty by the time people realize how successful the product has become and introduce similar concepts. Coca-Cola, for instance, was a first mover in 1886 and although Pepsi took its sweet time before following in the footsteps of Coca-Cola after 13 years, it is still playing catch up more than 100 years later.

Benefits of Being a First Mover

There are a few different first mover advantages, which help entrench a company in its particular industry. The first organization to introduce a new concept or product doesn't have to invest resources against competing products and can focus its marketing efforts on the benefits it offers. Since no other organization is offering a similar product, a first mover has ample time to make an impactful impression on consumers to build strong brand recognition and high levels of customer loyalty. Any consumer wishing to try this new concept has no choice, but to try the option made available via the first mover.

As other parties catch on to the popularity of a product or service and realize the profit-making opportunity, the first mover is already gaining in technical experience and consumer preferences. While others work on creating a similar product, the first mover can work on an updated version, which is in-tune with consumer needs. The organization also gains key marketing information, such as target markets, advertising strategies, which work well with the product, and so on. By the time a competing product or service is available, the first mover will be introducing version 2.0 and others will be following far behind.

Another possible advantage is that the first mover might be able to gain a strong control over raw material and other resources required to manufacture the object or deliver the service. They might occupy a key location in the distribution channel, sign contracts to control the chain of distribution, develop important contacts with key suppliers, or retain the top talent in the industry. Companies following in their shadow will have to spend additional time and resources to pry open distribution channels and build the same contracts.

One of the most coveted benefits of being a first mover in any industry is the opportunity to gain substantial advantage over others due to the high cost of converting clients from one brand to another. A generally accepted marketing concept states the cost of "stealing" customers from other brands is more expensive than generating new clients because you have to spend money convincing satisfied customers they will have an enhanced experience with your enterprise.

Consumers are generally risk-averse, meaning they will stick with a brand if they are satisfied with it. Even though a newer product may provide greater benefits, consumers are unwilling to risk trying the new product, as it may not satisfy their requirements as the older version. Once customers trust a product, they will select it over unfamiliar options, even if the product they purchase is more expensive.

When Are First Movers Successful?

There are a couple of circumstances, which are well suited to first movers and increase their chances of success. A market pioneer can be successful if the expected lifecycle of a product is extremely limited since he can jump ahead in the race early on and the finish line is too close to allow any competitor to even bother trying to play catch up. For instance, if you have created a new fashion style, it is likely it will have a short lifecycle based on the history of the industry.

Another situation when a first entrant can likely be successful is when a product's benefits are more subjective than objective. Dom Pérignon was a market pioneer in the champagne industry and the name is now viewed as a prestigious label, even though subsequent champagne brands may have been able to brew a similar or better tasting drink. In this case, the advantages gained by being a first mover are more difficult to dislodge by competitors since the product's qualities are highly subjective.

When a first mover can be reasonably assured of being granted patent or copyright protection for their innovation, the chances of being successful swell significantly. This is not to say others will not copy them eventually, but patent and copyright laws can grant the first entrant a few additional years to overcome mistakes, technological hurdles and build their brand image with consumers. The penalty late movers face at the start line will be sufficient to permit market pioneers to build an almost insurmountable lead over their competitors.

Successful First Movers

As mentioned earlier, Coca-Cola was a first mover that is holding on to that advantage even a hundred years after starting its operations, granted that the market share is a lot more dispersed now then in the late 1800's.

An example of a first mover advantage process rather than a product is that of Richard Arkwright who created the modern factory system after copying his idea from other processes already existing at the time. Mr. Arkwright developed a mechanized method to spin yarn and built his own factories and marketed the idea to a number of yarn factories already in operation.

Even though six years after his invention, his patent expired and people started copying his system, Mr. Arkwright had already gained a dominant position in the industry and built technical know-how which his competitors did not. His competitors tried to overlap him, but could not catch up to him long after his retirement.

Some may argue the above two stories are a bit outdated and with rapid diffusion of knowledge and technological prowess, it's difficult to gain the type of advantage these early corporations built, so let's study two more quick examples from more recent history.

Sony, the Japanese electronics manufacturer, set up shop after the Second World War and has become a global leader in the electronic and digital worlds. Their growth and success was due to their first mover philosophy. Sony's legendary founder, Ibuka Masaru, had one reason for his new company to exist, and it was to develop products and services, which nobody else was capable or willing to do. His successor at Sony, Morita Akio, added the other important part of this philosophy, which was to bring break-through technological products to market faster than the competition.

An even more recent example of a successful first mover who has hung on to the advantages they gained is eBay. No other online auction site comes anywhere close to the online auction business generated by eBay and the company has expanded vastly by offering other types of sales as well.

Pfizer's pharmaceutical drug to help men with erectile dysfunction, Viagra, is an excellent example of a first mover product, which gained enormous success. Although this was a new product in the prescription drug industry, Pfizer did not have to spend many resources convincing consumers this is a product they need to use. The need in society for a solution to erectile dysfunction was already immense and Viagra only had to tap that need. Viagra was further protected early on by the high cost of research, which is required to develop a drug approved by government health officials and by filing patents for their drug.

Difficulties Encountered by First Movers

We don't want to paint a picture that all first movers achieve success. Many of them fail because the timing for their product is not right or face technological hurdles that they cannot overcome. There are a number of disadvantages of being a first mover which you should be aware of in order to sidestep them on your path to success.

Sometimes, a product idea is so new to consumers that instead of marketing the product, first movers must convince consumers there is a need for their product. This puts an economic burden on the first entrant in an industry, which subsequent followers do not face and who can then target their budgets to simply marketing their product or service.

New technologies or services take time to develop and being the first to implement something means you do not have others to learn from so you make mistakes and adapt to the environment. These mistakes will cost you in terms of capital and brand loyalty (if there is a serious manufacturing issue with your product).

Those who follow avoid these expensive mistakes and develop better products and consumers dealing with these companies may rave about the quality of their service or product creating a buzz in the market about the follower rather than the first mover. Followers may also be able to improve on processes used before them and thus increase efficiencies in manufacturing and reduce production costs.

First movers may see the huge potential the market has to offer and since no other options are available in the market, they may feel they have a lot of time to establish themselves and fulfill consumer demands, so they will invest heavily in capital equipment. In reality, followers may already be eyeing their market and time their jump into the market to coincide with the availability of new technologies, giving the production capabilities a competitive advantage over first movers.

The belief that being the first entrant in an industry will lead to great benefits might compel an organization to jump the gun to win the race, but it may not be entirely ready, causing it to fail and the follower to pick up all the sales and benefits.

These disadvantages are well documented in the business world, so if your idea will make you a first mover, you can analyze the risks associated with each and develop countermeasures to ensure you avoid these roadblocks.

Fast Followers

The theory of first mover advantage was made popular in the late in 1980s in a study conducted at Stanford Business School. The theory gained wide acceptance as it intuitively made sense to people. Enter a market first and reap all the benefits. Subsequent research, however, has failed to show first movers have a wide scale advantage over other entrants in the industry or product category, particularly fast followers or as they are alternatively known, second movers or early market leaders.

Research

In a 1993 study cited in the prestigious Harvard Business Review, Peter N. Golder and Gerard J. Tellis, conducted a detailed analysis of new entrants in an industry. The authors observed 500 brands in 50 markets before concluding 47% of first movers fail versus an 8% failure rate for fast followers. The data was even more damning when the researchers highlighted the average market share among the first movers who did survive was lower than reported in previous papers.

Their observations also showed second movers have better long-term success than organizations that outpaced them in entering the market, even though on average the early market leaders in the study entered the industry over a decade later (13 years) after market pioneers. Ironically, the originators of the first mover theory, David Montgomery and Marvin Lieberman, retracted some of their conclusions in a study they published in 1998, a decade after the original paper.

Yet, the theory had captivated entrepreneurial minds for 10 years already and it had sunk too deep in the business world psyche to be undone so easily. The first mover theory fueled the dot-com bubble of the late 1990s as venture capitalists tripped over each other in the race to bring to fruition a new idea on the Internet. History revealed spending enormous amounts of money to be a market pioneer will not always lead to guaranteed success.

In this context, organizations should not be aiming be the first to enter new markets or launch new products as it becomes more of a race to fail first rather than a race to gain a competitive advantage over late-entrant competitors. Startups may need to realize being the second, fourth, fifth or even twelfth entrant in a market may not prevent them from becoming an industry leader and gain a substantial market share from earlier entrants.

Second Mover Advantages

Golder and Tellis's 1993 study suggests 47% of fast movers fail, but conversely this implies 53% of them succeed in entrepreneurship, which is actually a great accomplishment, unless you realize 92% of second movers are successful. Which group would you want to place your bets on? If you have an idea you have copied and improved upon, you are most likely already part of the late entrant group by default. It may be a chance for you to rejoice at your upcoming success, but before you party too much, it may be best to analyze why early market fast followers achieve this high level of success to allow you to duplicate the winning strategy with your copied innovation.

Often, innovators spend a lot of their finances on creating the product they bring to market, but by the time they are ready to launch, their capital resources are limited and they are moderately successful. A fast follower usually can observe the limited success of the first mover and enter the market with deeper pockets to promote their version of the product and gain a larger market share.

A late entrant company who merely replicates a market pioneer without introducing any innovative features is unlikely to gain much traction in the marketplace since it does not offer anything new to which customers are likely to gravitate. Conversely, an innovative fast follower can redefine a product category with substantial improvements made after studying the first generation of a product and even though they have entered the market later can reap the advantages of a first mover and fast follower.

When Are Fast Followers Successful?

The probability of success is higher for late entrants when a product has objective features, which can be measured. In this case, a product manufactured by a second mover can scientifically claim they have an enhanced version, for example specifications such as hard drive memory, RAM and processor speed help identify which laptop is more powerful. In such a situation, it is noticeably easier for early market leaders to convince consumers to give their product a try since they objectively have better specifications.

Another scenario in which late entrants can be successful is when the cost of replicating and slightly improving a product is lower than the cost of developing the product. If a product has no patent protection, for example, the costs to replicate it will be considerably lower than the original research and production costs.

Fast followers can also gain an advantage when market pioneers have spent extensive time and money educating consumers about the benefits of a product and have created the need for it. Fast followers can skip this step and save the vast capital resources it would require, leaving them better prepared for the upcoming battle with a first mover.

An excellent example is that of the prescription drug Zantac, which was launched by Glaxo after a few other pharmaceutical drug companies had already put out their ulcer-relief medication. Glaxo was able to concentrate their marketing efforts convincing consumers about the medical superiority of their drug instead of educating customers about the advantages of taking over-the-counter ulcer-relief pills.

The premise then that innovators, the first to offer a new service or product or the first to utilize a new process, will be successful may need to be modified to state the greatest innovation plan is to discover terrific new concepts in the market, rapidly copy and enhance them before marketing them. In other words, innovation by copying others will lead you to greater success than innovation itself.

Successful Fast Followers

Forbes' annual list of billionaires is unveiled with much fanfare every year, but the usual suspect at the top remains Bill Gates (worth $79.2 billion in the 2015 list). The company he founded, Microsoft, embodies the best and most convincing example of the advantages of being a fast follower. Microsoft has minted money with this philosophy over the years with the technologies it has unleashed upon consumers.

This is a company, which has made billions in profits based on the simple concept that it is best to wait, identify a popular product, innovate certain features, and reintroduce the product to the market. Think of Windows vs. Mac OS, Internet Explorer vs. Netscape, Word vs. WordPerfect and Excel vs. Lotus.

Experts are continuously harping about how Apple and Google have left Microsoft in their dust in the mobile and web development niches respectively. Although one has to admit Microsoft seems far behind, this is a company which has made a fortune out of copying and improving upon already successful ideas so it would not be fair to count them out of any race no matter how much of a lead the frontrunners may have over this (slow) fast follower corporation. Watch out Bing detractors. It may yet rise in the search engine industry!

Many people view Amazon.com as a market pioneer in online retailing, failing to realize a Wall Street executive was the first to launch an online bookstore. During the Internet's heyday in the early 1990s, Charles M. Stack, founded and launched Book Stacks Unlimited's online website books.com. Stack promoted his website on thousands of other websites and became quite successful, dominating the business for a number of years before the advent of Amazon.com. The second

mover though was able to improve on the online book pur-
chasing experience and eventually became the largest online
retailer in the US and an S&P 100 company.

Another illustration, which without doubt will be met with a
resounding consensus regarding the success achieved by a late
entrant in an industry, is Google. The World Wide Web is lit-
erally a labyrinth of data, which can be difficult to navigate
to access the information you need. This created the need for
online search engines and there were many online companies
dedicated to providing this service, yet no one did it better
than Google before or after its launch. Excite, AltaVista and
Yahoo Search all gained some recognition as search engines,
but were soon outdated when Google stepped into the market
with programming and algorithms, which produced faster and
better search results than the competition.

A final example which not only demonstrates the success of
being a fast follower, but also the advantages of copying an
existing product, improving it and re-launching it as your own
invention is Facebook. Rumors persist Mark Zuckerberg took
his idea from a couple of college friends and whether that is
accurate or not is not our concern. In reality, Facebook itself
was an improved imitation of pre-existing social media networks, such as Friendster and MySpace, both of which had
initial success only to be quickly supplanted by Facebook,
which is now viewed as a first mover even though it clearly is
not one.

As a second mover it was able to avoid all the pitfalls encoun-
tered by a market pioneer, yet Facebook now reaps the advantages that first movers gain. For instance, references and links
to a new entrant in the social media industry, tsū.co, with a
revolutionary new idea of paying its members a part of the
advertising revenue they help generate (currently Facebook

pays nothing at all to the people who sign on to use its plat-form) have all been deleted from every Facebook member profiles.

You cannot talk about it, link it, comment on it or promote this new company on Facebook. Tsu.co will have to put in the effort to cut its own cake if it wants to have a bite to eat. The tsū.co team does seem ready to creatively take on the challenge, creating their Facebook profile under the name tsu-dotco, to outsmart Facebook's censoring measures. The lesson here is that even top brands, products, services and processes can be challenged if you are creative and innovative enough.

5

Innovation is (Not) Stealing

The examples of the Apple's mouse, GUI, iPad and the World Wide Web along with the discussion about first mover versus fast follower was designed to demonstrate the greater chances of success a person or organization has when they copy an idea before improving it slightly and bringing it to market.

First Mover Myth

It's time to revisit a couple of the examples of successful first movers to dispel a myth left lingering purposely to help you critically appreciate the vast benefits "copycats" have over people with brand new ideas.

Coca-Cola is a first mover, which has managed to keep its competitive advantage over an impressive 100 years. This is not by fluke, as the company has constantly worked and designed innovative marketing strategies to keep its brand image fresh in the minds of consumers. The late entrant, Pepsi, has not been able to dislodge Coca-Cola from owning the biggest piece of the market share pie. As of May 2015, Forbes reports Coca-Cola has a market cap of almost $180 billion versus a market cap of "only" $143 billion for PepsiCo. Granted PepsiCo is not worth more than Coca-Cola, but no one will argue this fast mover hasn't been successful in establishing itself and earning big bucks.

In our other example, we highlighted the first mover philosophy adopted by Sony and which helped propel this technology company to remarkable heights. The company, which was founded in 1946, has no doubt become a world leader in consumer electronics with annual sales approaching $77 billion. Yet, founded in 1969, Samsung Electronics is a late entrant, especially given it was initially in the semiconductors business before eventually finding its fame in consumer electronics, can claim greater success than Sony. Forbes reported Samsung Electronics is among the top 10 companies in the world in terms of market capitalization and has annual sales around $200 billion.

In both cases, there is no denying the first movers have been successful, but with the success demonstrated by the above two early market leaders and the added knowledge that 92% of fast followers are successful, doesn't it make a lot more sense to hedge your bets on a "stolen" and reintroduced idea? The myth we want to shatter is if a fast mover encounters immense success, it does not mean the marketplace does not have space for an innovative late entrant.

Myth of Single Inventor Creations

A majority of inventions in history appear to take an evolutionary road: radio, television, the Internet, cars, planes, and satellites, all appear to be the work of several "genius" minds working on an evolutionary path to make subsequent improvements to get to a final product, which will also continue to undergo continuous modifications as technologies improve. Even apparently single inventor products, like the telephone and light bulb, were the result of a serial accumulation of discoveries and knowledge, which led to a breakthrough. Several minor and major inventions over a period of time are crucial for "innovation" to take place.

This concept of a magical light moment or the belief that innovation is the result of an epiphany or comes from serendipity is far from the real state of affairs. Good (and profitable) concepts have to normally grind their way through a sequence of enhancements as people with different experiences, goals, perspectives and ideas come across them, but one has to admit it takes a special kind of mind to unite the dots from different disciplines to create amazing possibilities.

A Final Word

This book aims to inspire you to change how you view things around you. You may have a career in a particular field, which has provided you some sort of expertise. Even if that career is simply an administrative one, there are always processes, services and products, which can be refined. All you have to do is change the belief that many people hold, consciously or not, that innovation is beyond their capabilities.

Innovation can be, and really is copying an existing idea and improving upon it. Have you ever been frustrated by something? Instead of open criticism, take a moment to think how the situation could be improved. This simple change in your thought process can provide you with the stimulus you need to eventually make a profitable innovation.

Also keep the business side of things in mind. A profitable idea may not always lead you to money (others might end up profiting more than you do from your idea). This is a cut-throat world so once you have an idea, take steps to protect it, whether it is waiting to move ahead as a fast follower or meeting with a lawyer to protect your brainchild.

Don't just jump head in, but take the time to consult appropriate people and get advice. Experience (and if you don't have it then advice from experienced people) is necessary for bringing your idea successfully to consumers. Before you get going, you will need a comprehensive business plan, including financing, marketing and production strategies.

The purpose of the book was to demonstrate the simplicity and utter genius in revisiting and innovating old ideas. It is absolutely false that everything of value already exists in the marketplace. You need to reject the thought that innovation is stealing and open your mind to the endless possibilities there exists to copy and improve on all sorts of things around you and make a fortune while doing so and we hope to have inspired you to make this your goal.

www.ingramcontent.com/pod-product-compliance
Lightning Source LLC
Chambersburg PA
CBHW070409190526
45169CB00003B/1181